The Graceful Bull
and Other Surprises

by Cynthia Carroll
illustrated by Michael David

≋Harcourt

Orlando   Boston   Dallas   Chicago   San Diego

Visit *The Learning Site!*

www.harcourtschool.com

The English language is full of words and expressions that have colorful and interesting histories.

The word *hamburger*, for example, is usually said to be named after the city of Hamburg, Germany. People who say this believe that the hamburger was invented in Germany.

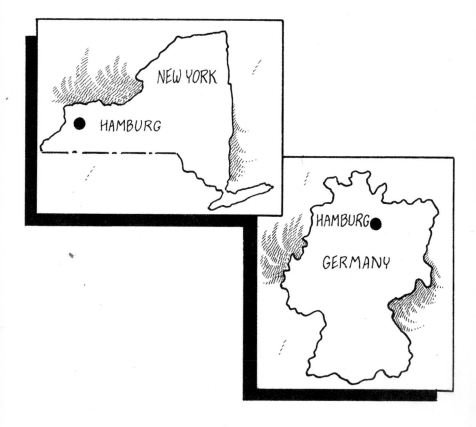

However, the people in the town of Hamburg, New York, claim that it was invented there. They say that the first hamburger was served during the summer of 1885 by Charles and Frank Menches, who were from Ohio. They had a food stand at the Erie County Fair, which was held in Hamburg. When they ran out of pork, they decided to serve ground beef patties instead.

But no matter where the hamburger was invented, you won't hear it called anything but a hamburger, or *burger* for short.

This is not so with the frankfurter. Although you won't hear it called a *furter*, it is often referred to as a *frank* or a *hot dog*. Have you ever wondered why we call frankfurters *hot dogs*?

Hot dogs were not given that name by the person who invented them. Nor were they named that by anyone who sold them. Here's what happened.

It was about the year 1900. A man named Harry Stevens, who had a food stand in Coney Island, New York, was the first to serve grilled franks on a split roll, otherwise known as a bun. On cold days he and his workers would call out, "Get your red hots!"

T. A. Dorgan, a sports cartoonist with a reputation for being clever, drew the frankfurter as a dachshund dog on a roll. He called it the hot dog. What gave him the idea might have been the fact that many people thought that franks were made of dog meat! The people who made them, of course, would probably have taken an oath that they were not.

In any case, the name *hot dog* stuck. Now you are more likely to hear them called hot dogs than frankfurters.

Of course, anyone from the "upper crust," who would have been completely absorbed with themselves and concerned about others' opinions about them, probably would never have eaten a hot dog. And that brings us to another interesting phrase: *upper crust*. Where did that come from? What does it mean?

In the mid-1400s, it was considered good manners to cut off the upper crust of a loaf of bread and offer it to your most honored guest. It was best if you did this with a beaming smile on your face. This would show that you were happy to do it.

You must remember that loaves of bread were homemade in those days. They were not packaged and already cut into slices. After a loaf was baked, you would cut it yourself. The top crust was considered to be the best part of the loaf. If you didn't offer the upper crust to your guest, you might get the reputation of being a bad host.

Getting a bad reputation might really *take the wind out of your sails*. In other words, it might really slow you down, socially at least. This interesting statement comes to us from pirates.

When pirates wanted to board a merchant ship, they often sailed to the windward side of the ship. Doing this cut off the wind blowing on the other ship's sails and slowed it down. Then the pirates could easily board the merchant ship.

Today, when we say that something takes the wind out of our sails, we mean that it slows us down or makes us feel bad. For example, you might say that you had the wind knocked out of your sails if you did not make the basketball team or you did poorly on a test that you had studied hard for. That would certainly change a beaming smile to a sad frown. It would also sidetrack you from carrying out any plans you had made.

That brings us to the word *sidetrack*. Where did it come from? Well, in railroad terms, there are main tracks and side tracks. Sometimes it is necessary to sidetrack a car or a group of cars. This enables another train to get through on the main track.

Thus, someone who is sidetracked has been turned aside from his or her main purpose. For example, you might get sidetracked if the phone rings as you are walking out the door to meet a friend. If you are late, you might tell your friend that you got "sidetracked."

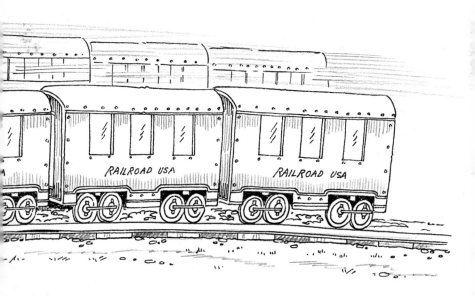

If you manage to keep on track, however, you could keep on going *like a house on fire*. This interesting statement began on the western frontier in the 1700s.

In those days, log cabins were common. They were very practical because they were made out of common materials that were easy to find. The

only problem was that they would burn very quickly if they caught fire.

A pioneer who saw a horse running across the prairie might have said, "He can run like a house on fire." This meant that the horse was very fast. The phrase *like a house on fire* still means "very quickly" or "with lots of energy."

Of course, "very quickly" is one way you wouldn't want a *bull in a china shop* to move. This interesting statement has been part of our language since the early 1800s. Anyone who is said to be a bull in a china shop is thought to be clumsy and careless. The statement certainly makes you think of a very bad combination: bulls and china just don't seem like a good mix!

Curiously, the following story seems to question the accuracy of the idea that a bull would destroy a china shop. In 1936, the bandleader Fred Waring made a bet with actor Paul Douglas. The bandleader lost the bet. As his penalty, he had to lead a bull through Plummer's China Shop in New York City. Waring had to take an oath that he would pay for any china that might get broken.

That bull walked up the first aisle, and nothing happened. Then it walked down the second aisle, and still nothing happened. The bull was led through the entire china shop, and it did not break so much as a teacup!

However, the bandleader must have been absorbed in his thoughts because he didn't seem to be paying much attention. He knocked over a whole table of china. Maybe the statement should be changed to a *bandleader in a china shop!*